TIGER WOODS

A Real-Life Reader Biography

John Torres

Mitchell Lane Publishers, Inc.
P.O. Box 619
Bear, Delaware 19701

Mitchell Lane
PUBLISHERS

Second Printing

Real-Life Reader Biographies

Paula Abdul	Christina Aguilera	Marc Anthony	Lance Armstrong
Drew Barrymore	Tony Blair	Brandy	Garth Brooks
Kobe Bryant	Sandra Bullock	Mariah Carey	Aaron Carter
Cesar Chavez	Roberto Clemente	Christopher Paul Curtis	Roald Dahl
Oscar De La Hoya	Trent Dimas	Celine Dion	Sheila E.
Gloria Estefan	Mary Joe Fernandez	Michael J. Fox	Andres Galarraga
Sarah Michelle Gellar	Jeff Gordon	Mia Hamm	Melissa Joan Hart
Salma Hayek	Jennifer Love Hewitt	Faith Hill	Hollywood Hogan
Katie Holmes	Enrique Iglesias	Allen Iverson	Janet Jackson
Derek Jeter	Steve Jobs	Alicia Keys	Michelle Kwan
Bruce Lee	Jennifer Lopez	Cheech Marin	Ricky Martin
Mark McGwire	Alyssa Milano	Mandy Moore	Chuck Norris
Tommy Nuñez	Rosie O'Donnell	Mary-Kate and Ashley Olsen	Rafael Palmeiro
Gary Paulsen	Colin Powell	Freddie Prinze, Jr.	Condoleezza Rice
Julia Roberts	Robert Rodriguez	J.K. Rowling	Keri Russell
Winona Ryder	Cristina Saralegui	Charles Schulz	Arnold Schwarzenegger
Selena	Maurice Sendak	Dr. Seuss	Shakira
Alicia Silverstone	Jessica Simpson	Sinbad	Jimmy Smits
Sammy Sosa	Britney Spears	Julia Stiles	Ben Stiller
Sheryl Swoopes	Shania Twain	Liv Tyler	Robin Williams
Vanessa Williams	Venus Williams	**Tiger Woods**	

Library of Congress Cataloging-in-Publication Data
Torres, John Albert.

Tiger Woods/John Torres.
p. cm. — (A real-life reader biography)
Includes index.
ISBN 1-58415-067-X
1. Woods, Tiger — Juvenile literature. 2. Golfers—United States—Biography—Juvenile literature. 3. Racially mixed people—United States—Biography—Juvenile literature. [1. Woods, Tiger. 2. Golfers. 3. Racially mixed people—Biography.] I Title. II. Series.
GV964.W66 T67 2001
796.352'092—dc21
[B]
00-067659

ABOUT THE AUTHOR: John A. Torres is the assistant city editor for the Poughkeepsie Journal newspaper. He has written more than 20 sports biographies including Oscar De La Hoya (Enslow), Kevin Garnett (Lerner), and several for Mitchell Lane. He lives in Fishkill, New York with his wife and two children. When not writing, John likes to fish, coach youth sports, and spend time with his family.

DEDICATION: This book is dedicated to my wife and children who support me whenever I try to open new doors, and to people like Tiger Woods who have succeeded in opening new doors.

PHOTO CREDITS: cover: Paul Sanders/Archive Photos; p. 4 Kirby Lee/The Sporting Image; pp. 7, 9 Archive Photos; p. 10 Marin & Associates; p. 13 Archive Photos; p. 14 Allsport; pp. 21, 25, 27, 28 Archive Photos.

ACKNOWLEDGMENTS: The following story has been thoroughly researched, and to the best of our knowledge, represents a true story. While every possible effort has been made to ensure accuracy, the publisher will not assume liability for damages caused by inaccuracies in the data, and makes no warranty on the accuracy of the information contained herein. This story has not been authorized nor endorsed by Tiger Woods.

Table of Contents

Chapter 1
The Moment

Tiger Woods did not invent golf. It only seems like he did.

Everyone remembers the moment too; the moment when Tiger Woods stormed onto the golf scene and claimed the sport for his own. On a warm, overcast spring day in April 1997, 21-year-old Tiger broke every barrier, every stereotype, every racist roadblock, and delivered one of the greatest golfing performances ever.

It was the annual Masters golf tournament, held in Augusta, Georgia, at a club that only started letting black

Tiger Woods did not invent golf. It only seems like he did.

"He's more dominant over the guys he's playing against than I ever was over the ones I played against," said Jack Nicklaus.

men play golf there in 1991. The greatest golfers in the world were assembled to compete for the title of Masters Champion and the privilege of wearing the famous green jacket that is given to the winner every year. Tom Kite, Nick Faldo, and Greg Norman were among the many elite players who would soon learn that Tiger was more than just a nickname.

Tiger Woods so dominated the tournament that he left his elder competitors in awe. Even golfing legends were left scratching their heads at Tiger's performance.

"He's more dominant over the guys he's playing against than I ever was over the ones I played against," said hall-of-fame golfer Jack Nicklaus.

Nearly all professional golf tournaments last four days, with golfers playing 18 holes each day. On Saturday, the next to last day, Tiger sank an amazing seven birdies to help him simply destroy the competition. He went on to win the Masters by 12

strokes as he finished an incredible 18 shots under par.

Par is the golf term for the number of strokes a golfer is expected to use to sink the golf ball into each hole. A birdie is the term used if the golfer is able to sink the ball one shot below par. For example, a golfer is credited with a birdie if he needs only four shots on a par-5 hole.

His performance was made even more spectacular because the Augusta National Course is regarded as just about the toughest golf course to play in the world. In fact, most golfers are satisfied with a par performance. Yet Tiger was 18 strokes below par, which meant he needed only 270 strokes. That was a Masters tournament record, as no one had ever finished all four days using so few strokes.

But it wasn't just a great performance in his first major tournament as a professional golfer that put the name Tiger Woods in just about every household in America. No, it was also due in part to the huge following that he suddenly gained. Halfway through the tournament, thousands of spectators began following him around the course, watching his every move. And it was also the highest-rated golf tournament in television history. Men, women and children, many of whom had never previously bothered to watch golf on television, were suddenly glued to their

Tiger celebrates his final putt after he won the PGA Championship at Medinah Country Club, August 15, 1999.

sets watching, rooting, and pulling for a 21-year-old minority to win.

But Tiger Woods' widespread popularity was also due to a certain sound, or rather the lack of that sound, throughout the country. The sound of doors slamming in the faces of black children everywhere at golf courses and country clubs seemed to stop. Tiger Woods had opened those doors for everyone.

Another thing that made Tiger's dominating performance so exceptional

Tiger graciously autographs a hat for one of his many fans.

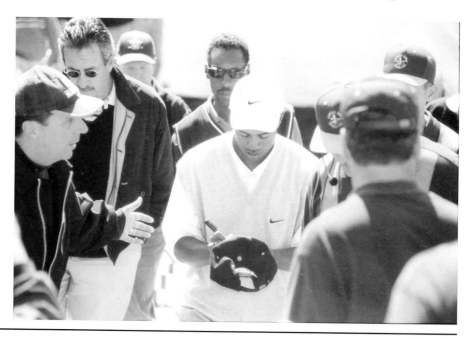

— for those who did not know him —
was that every night after playing golf
he would eat burgers and fries with his
friends, play table tennis and basketball,
and stay up late playing video games.
He didn't seem the least bit nervous.

After sinking a five-foot putt to finish
the tournament and set his scoring
records, Tiger sent his right fist in a
mock uppercut toward the sky, a move
that would become his trademark.

Soon a jubilant Tiger was awarded
the green jacket, which defending
champion Nick Faldo helped him put
on. Tiger, wearing a bright red shirt and
sporting a band-aid on his right hand
from blisters, could not help but laugh.
It was a dream come true.

Tiger hugged his caddie and then
went looking for his mother and father.
Exhausted, he fell into his father's arms
and cried tears of joy.

People would have to get used to
seeing the hugs and tears and that
celebratory uppercut move.

Tiger Woods was here to stay.

Tiger never seems nervous during a pro tourna-ment.

Chapter 2
Little Tiger

Tiger's real name is Eldrick Woods.

The fact that 21-year old Tiger Woods had won what many people say is the most important golf tournament in America at such a young age hardly came as a surprise to his parents. After all, it almost seemed as if Tiger was born with a golf club in his hand.

Eldrick "Tiger" Woods was born on December 30, 1975, in Cypress, California, near Los Angeles. Right from the start Tiger was unique. His father Earl was African-American and his mother Kultida was from Thailand, meaning Tiger was a rare combination of black and Asian.

Earl was a retired lieutenant colonel in the United States Army and he befriended a Vietnamese soldier named Vuong Dang Phong during the Vietnam War. Earl was impressed by the courage that Phong possessed and immediately starting calling him Tiger. He told his friend that if he ever had a son he would nickname him Tiger as well. So from the moment his son was born, Earl called him Tiger.

Tiger's mother, Kultida, is a native of Thailand. She impressed the philosophies of the Orient, stressing peace of mind and a tranquil mentality, on Tiger. She has even taken Tiger with her on several occasions to her homeland to visit ancient temples, study religion and philosophy and just be exposed to the culture. That is why

Tiger's father, Earl, shows his new book, Training a Tiger, *at a book signing in May 1997.*

Tiger never seems out of sorts, aggravated, or upset on the golf course. Win or lose, he always looks the same.

Tiger is very proud of both his parents' culture and heritage. In fact, he sometimes gets agitated when he is referred to as African-American. He argues that he is an American of Oriental and African-American ancestry.

By the time he was six months old, Tiger seemed to have golf on his mind.

Tiger, shown here with his mother, Kultida, displays his trophy for the 100th U.S. Open, June 18, 2000, Pebble Beach, CA.

He would sometimes watch as his father Earl would hit golf balls into a net. Soon after, Tiger's parents caught him imitating his father's golf swing.

It didn't take him long to become a child wonder regarding golf. He watched it on television, he talked about it, and he began playing as soon as he could. Earl, noticing his son's interest, simply fed Tiger's hunger to learn more about the sport. He taught him the history as well as the technical stuff.

That meant that Tiger not only knew how to grip and swing a golf club, but also who the all-time great golfers were. His father also taught him about the great black golfers who never got the chance to play in the major tournaments. He learned about Lee Elder, who at 39 was finally allowed to win a PGA (Professional Golfer's Association) event. He was the first black man ever allowed to play in the Masters, in 1975, the year Tiger was born. He also learned all about Teddy Rhodes and Charlie Sifford, who were never even given the chance.

Tiger's father, Earl, taught him all about golf when he was just a youngster.

In fact, when Tiger won the Masters, he spotted Elder on the course and ran over to greet him. He hugged the golfing legend and thanked him for opening the doors for people like himself. Some people said that Elder had tears in his eyes.

By the time Tiger was a toddler, he was a good golfer. He appeared on the Mike Douglas show at age two, putting with Bob Hope.

Tiger also learned about his father. Earl had been the first black man ever allowed to play baseball in college's Big Eight Conference, but he was often forced to stay in separate hotels and eat at separate restaurants than his white teammates. On the field of play all the men were viewed as equals. But once they walked off the field and into the real world, it was different.

So Tiger grew up knowing all the stories about racial prejudice. He also knew that maybe he would be the one to change things.

They say that the famous composer Mozart wrote an opera before he was five years old. Well, in his own way, Tiger was becoming the Mozart of the golf course.

He was always on the course with his father. He would practice and perfect his swing. By the time he was a toddler, the swing and movements of a golfer seemed natural.

As a child wonder, Tiger was such a good golfer that he actually appeared on the Mike Douglas television show at the age of two, putting with Bob Hope, the famous comedian and golfing fan. By the time he was three, Tiger shot an incredible 48 for nine holes at a local golf course. Two years later, he was being featured in the monthly magazine *Golf Digest*. He was a celebrity even before he knew what the word meant. As a little kid, Tiger was already starting to be famous.

As he grew older, Tiger became even better and more famous. He won the Optimist International Junior Tournament six times, at the ages of eight, nine, 12, 13, 14, and 15. Also at age 15, he became the youngest golfer to win the National Junior Championship. The next year, he was the first golfer to win that title twice. And no one was surprised when he won again at age 17 to become the only one to ever win it three times.

By this time, it was clear to people, little Tiger had grown and was ready to make his move.

At age five, Tiger was being featured in *Golf Digest*.

Chapter 3
Moving Up

With his mother's Asian teachings, Tiger has the right temperament to be successful in golf.

Golf is the kind of game that takes years of practice, even for a natural. It is the kind of game that forces serious players to spend hours at the driving range, hitting bucket after bucket of golf balls out into open fields. It's a game that makes players spend even more hours putting on the practice greens.

Many people throughout the world enjoy the sport of golf. But not many are serious enough to put in the required time it takes to perfect a swing or to learn the trick of putting a little spin on the ball to make it jump back toward the hole after landing beyond it. But Tiger was serious. He spent the time it took to perfect his golfing skills.

Due in part to his mother's Asian teachings and philosophies, Tiger also had the right temperament to be successful in golf. He was brought up to have a quiet determination and a strong drive to succeed. But he was also levelheaded and calm, blessed with a sort of inner peace.

The person with the biggest influence in Tiger's life was and still is his father, Earl. He taught Tiger the difference between right and wrong, and how a person's life is filled with many choices but not many chances.

Some of the advice he constantly repeated to his son included "Don't be a follower, be a leader" and "You know what's right and what's wrong. Do the right thing." This kind of advice helped Tiger stay out of trouble as a teenager.

It also helps Tiger's golf game that he stands six feet, two inches and weighed 180 pounds. He is therefore tall and slender, what golfers call having a

But the person with the biggest influence in Tiger's life was and still is his father.

When Tiger was 16, he played in his first professional tournament, the Nissan Los Angeles Open.

"long" body. That is the perfect body for being able to perfect the graceful motions that playing golf requires. He also has incredible strength, something he developed as a teenager. Tiger was always able to drive the ball off the tee further than any of his competitors and then beat them on the short game.

In 1992 at the age of 16, Tiger was able to play in his first professional tournament, the Nissan Los Angeles Open, and still keep his amateur status. Being an amateur meant that Tiger was not allowed to earn any money while playing golf. This was important because it ensured that Tiger would be able to participate on a college golf team and still be able to compete against well-known professional golfers.

He played in three more PGA events a year later and one of his best performances against professionals came in the 1994 Johnnie Walker Asian Classic in his mother's native country of Thailand. He finished in 34th place, which is considered very respectable.

But Tiger wasn't only about golf. Even though he was probably the world's best 17-year-old golfer, in many ways he was a typical teenager. When he wasn't practicing on the golf course or studying for school, Tiger loved to play video games with his friends. They would all take turns trying to master martial arts games like Mortal Kombat.

He also loved to mess around on the basketball court and enjoyed eating some of his favorite foods like pizza and tacos with his friends.

Tiger won the Asian Honda Classic in Bangkok, Thailand, February 9, 1997. His mother, who is from Thailand, is beside him.

Chapter 4
College Champion

Tiger had his pick of colleges when he graduated from Western High School in Anaheim, California.

Tiger had become such a well-known golfer as a teenager that he basically had his pick of colleges when he graduated from Western High School in Anaheim, California. College recruiters and coaches knew that having Tiger attend their school would ensure that their golf teams would compete for the national collegiate championship.

Tiger had a few specific things he was looking for while picking a school. He wanted a school in a warm-weather climate so he would be able to play golf all year. He also wanted one that was good academically. And just as important, he wanted a school close to home, close to his parents.

His choice was Stanford University and in September 1994, Tiger enrolled as a freshman. While he excelled in the classroom as an above-average student, Tiger did not disappoint on the golf course.

In the two years he spent at Stanford, Tiger won 10 collegiate events including the NCAA (National Collegiate Athletics Association) title. He also had the honor of representing the United States in the 1994 World Amateur Team Championships in France and the 1995 Walker Cup Match in Wales. Tiger was certainly gaining a lot of national and international exposure in the golf world.

Tiger also kept making a big impression in professional tournaments as an amateur. He participated in the Masters, the British Open and the Scottish Open. He also began the U.S. Open but a wrist injury forced him to withdraw.

Tiger chose Stanford University.

Tiger wanted to win all the amateur titles before he turned pro.

Many people were trying to convince Tiger to turn professional at that time. There was a lot of money to be made on the pro circuit. But he knew that he was not quite ready, though it was doubtful that he could wait all four years of college before turning pro. Tiger had one more goal to accomplish as an amateur before he would join the professional circuit — he wanted to win three consecutive national amateur titles.

After winning his third amateur title, there was little else Tiger could accomplish as an amateur. After all, he had been named the Golf Digest Amateur Player of the Year in 1991 and 1992, GolfWorld Amateur Player of the Year in 1992 and 1993, Golfweek National Amateur of the Year in 1991 and 1992, and GolfWorld "Man of the Year" in 1994. In addition, he was chosen for the Fred Haskins and Jack Nicklaus College Player of the Year awards in 1996.

So there were no other amateur titles for him to win. Tiger had already won them all. He also had played for several years among the world's best professionals and proven that he could hold his own. The time, therefore, had come for Tiger to leave college and begin playing professional golf.

Tiger's first tournament as a professional was the Greater Milwaukee Open in late August, 1996. Though he had a hole-in-one during one of his rounds, he finished only 60th. But a month later he won his first tournament by beating a much more experienced golfer in an 18-hole playoff. Two weeks later he won his second tournament, the Walt Disney Classic. What happened next is the stuff that legends are made of.

Tiger poses with Mickey Mouse after he won the National Car Rental Golf Classic on October 24, 1999. The tournment was played at the Walt Disney World Resort in Orlando, Florida.

Chapter 5
Superstar

By the time
Tiger was
24, he had
established
himself as
one of the
all-time
greatest
golfers.

Tiger's performance at the Masters served as a wake-up call to other golfers as well as a lightning rod that seemed to reinvigorate a sport which had rarely seen one player become so dominant so quickly.

By the time he was 24, Tiger had established himself as one of the all-time greatest golfers. In just under four years, Tiger had claimed 29 tournaments, including 23 on the PGA tour.

He had matched the record of golfing legend Ben Hogan set in 1953 by winning three professional major championships in the same year. He also became the first golfer since Denny Shute in 1936-37 to win the PGA Championship in consecutive years.

But perhaps Tiger's most impressive showing, the one tournament that simply left others scratching their heads and wondering if they would ever be able to beat Tiger, was his victory at the 100th U.S. Open in June 2000.

He won the four-day tournament by 15 strokes, which was the widest winning margin at a major tournament since Tom Morris at the 1862 British Open! People watching the tournament did not wonder whether Tiger would win. No, they wondered how much he would win by!

Tiger jokes with his coach Buch Harmon during a practice round at St. Andrews, July 17, 2000, in a qualifying round for the 129th British Open.

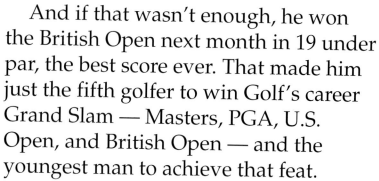

And if that wasn't enough, he won the British Open next month in 19 under par, the best score ever. That made him just the fifth golfer to win Golf's career Grand Slam — Masters, PGA, U.S. Open, and British Open — and the youngest man to achieve that feat.

But all of Tiger's success is due to one thing — hard work. He is so dedicated that on the eve of the tournament he was seen practicing on the greens even though he was already putting much better than nearly any other golfer there.

Tiger with girl-friend Joanna Jagoda at the official ceremony for the Presidents Cup at Royal Melbourne Golf Club, December 13, 1998.

"I didn't like the way I was rolling the ball," Tiger said. "The ball wasn't turning over quite the way I would like to see it roll. I worked on it for a couple of hours and found that my posture was a little off. My release was a little off."

It is doubtful that there is another golfer with Tiger's

work ethic. He is constantly practicing, tinkering, and perfecting his swing. It is what has helped make him so great. In fact, it has even become a point of contention with some golfers. Many criticized him for not personally paying tribute to golfer Payne Stewart, who was killed in a 1999 plane crash. While many of the nation's top golfers attended a memorial service for Stewart, Tiger was on the course practicing.

But after the U.S. Open, other golfers — great players in their own right — could do nothing but sing Tiger's praises.

"Tiger has raised the bar," said golf great Tom Watson, "and it seems that he's the only guy who can jump over that bar."

Tiger seems to know his place in history, even for one so young. He also knows that there are a lot of people looking at him, depending on him, and idolizing him. All this makes him realize the importance of giving back.

All of Tiger's success is due to hard work.

Even though Tiger's parents are now separated, Tiger remains close to both of them. His mother is often the one at the tournaments cheering him on loudly while Earl watches from a distance. After winning the U.S. Open title, Tiger told reporters that he couldn't wait to give it to his dad for a Father's Day gift.

Tiger is set for life. He has already earned so much money playing golf that he will never have to worry about his finances. His appealing face and good-natured personality have also made him a favorite among companies who have asked him to endorse their products. Tiger has lucrative endorsement contracts with Nike and several other companies.

But for Tiger it has never been about the money. Even his opponents recognize that.

"He's not playing for the money," said golf great Davis Love. "He thinks about winning and nothing else. I like the way he thinks."

Tiger has used some of his money to start the Tiger Woods Foundation to help young children, especially inner-city kids, succeed in life. Tiger and his dad go around the country showing kids how to swing a golf club. More importantly, they try to teach them that hard work and dedication, not violence and drugs, are the way to success. At a golf clinic in July 2000, Tiger's dad Earl delivered such an emotional speech that many parents and kids in attendance were in tears. They gave him a standing ovation.

The message is simple, but sometimes it means more to a kid when he hears it from his hero's mouth. Tiger loves to spend time with kids, answering their questions and trying to inspire them. It is clear that he really does care about children and how they view him. This attitude makes him different from some athletes, who shy away from being a role model.

But Tiger, like his nickname implies, doesn't shy away from anything.

Tiger set up the Tiger Woods Foundation to help inner-city kids succeed in life. Tiger likes being a role model.

Chronology

- 1975, born on December 30 in Cypress, California.
- 1978, appeared on television putting with comedian and golfer Bob Hope.
- 1992, played in Nissan Los Angeles Open at the age of 16, his first professional tournament.
- 1992, named Golf Digest Amateur Player of the Year for the second consecutive year.
- 1996, won his third consecutive U.S. Amateur title, then turned professional.
- 1996, selected by Sports Illustrated as the Sportsman of the Year.
- 1997, won the prestigious Masters Tournament.
- 1999, won the PGA Championship.
- 2000, won the U.S. Open; won the British Open; won the PGA Championship
- 2001, won the Masters Tournament; first player in modern golf history to win four straight professional major tournaments

Index